How to Get Started as a
Technical Writer

D0818400

How to Get Started as a Technical Writer

The practical, no-nonsense, real-world guide to preparing for and launching your career in technical writing

James Gill

How to Get Started as a Technical Writer

www.techsavvywriter.com

ISBN-13: 978-1475005035
ISBN-10: 1475005032

Contents

Who is This Book For?

If you're serious about starting a career in technical writing, I believe *How to Become a Technical Writer* is for you.

I wrote this book to answer the questions I've been asked hundreds of times in my 20-year career as a technical writer, like:

- What *is* technical writing, anyway?
- How do I get experience and land my first job?
- What are employers really looking for, and how do I get hired?
- What are the "must-have" skills for a technical writer?
- Should I get more education or training?

In the chapters that follow, I attempt to answer all those questions (and more) in practical ways that can help you prepare for and start a career in technical writing. It's the kind of book I wish I had when I began my career.

This is my view of the technical writing field, based on two decades of experience. Others will have different stories and advice. But I believe that what you'll find here applies to *anyone* interested in a career in technical writing—and who wants to get started *now*.

But before we go any further, I want to tell you two important things:

1: Technical writing isn't for everyone

Technical writing is a fantastic career field. It's rewarding, both financially and personally, and few careers offer as much opportunity to learn, grow, and work in diverse fields and industries.

But it comes with challenges—and the first one is breaking into the field in the first place. Most of all, being a technical writer requires a lot of confidence in yourself, and the flexibility to continually learn new things and adapt to changing needs and environments.

2: There are no magic formulas

Like any rewarding career, success is ultimately—and entirely—up to you. You're in charge. But if you're willing to stick with it and understand and apply the material here, I promise that you'll be better prepared than 99% of those you'll compete with for your first technical writing job.

Have I scared you off yet? Good. Let's get started!

How To Use This Book

This book assumes you already communicate well in your native language, both verbally and in writing. There is no substitute for this. It doesn't matter if English is your first or third language—as long as you're comfortable with your language and can use it to communicate clearly.

My goal is to provide tools and strategies that can help you prepare for and launch a career in technical writing. However, the key ingredient of this book is *you*; active participation is what will get results.

Each chapter builds on information in the previous chapter. If possible, read the chapters in order, from beginning to end. However, feel free to skip to any section you choose if you're looking for specific information.

To get the most out of this book, be sure to complete all the tasks in the *Do This* section at the end of each chapter. I recommend preparing a notebook or electronic document to keep notes, track your progress, and record the results of each chapter's exercises.

Do This

1. Get a notebook (or start an electronic document) to capture your notes and exercise results and track your progress.
2. Set a goal for yourself for completing the book and getting your first job. Make it explicit and fixed in time, and *write it down*. Don't worry if this changes later—the key is to set a goal and plan for how to reach it.

My Story

I never intended to become a technical writer.

I was going to be an electrical engineer. But in my first year of college, sweating through my second calculus course and praying for a passing grade, I realized—engineers are supposed to *love* math. I barely *liked* math.

I did love my writing and science courses, though, and was endlessly curious about how things worked. I helped friends and classmates fix computers and write their assignments, and I convinced the school paper to let me write articles.

So, at the end of my first year, I visited a career counselor. After a lot of thought and discussion, I did what any self-respecting former engineering major would do:

I majored in History and English.

Meanwhile, I kept building computers and writing articles for the school paper. One day, I saw an ad seeking temporary workers to test computer software. I applied, and got the job.

To my surprise, the best part of software testing was helping engineers to make products more user-friendly. I became the "go-to" person for writing test reports and recommendations. I found that I always got excited when explaining technology to other people. Though curious about how technology *worked*, I was even more fascinated about how people *used* it.

At the end of that job, I was hooked—technology was fun, I learned something new every day, and computers were evolving at breakneck speed. Encouraged by the experience, I joined the local chapter of the Society for Technical Communication and responded to an ad seeking someone to write manuals for an agricultural software product. I got the job, again.

And so began my accidental career in technical writing.

That first technical writing job was incredibly difficult. Half the time I didn't know what I was doing. I knew computers and page layout software and how to write well, but I had a lot to learn about juggling priorities and organizing my own tasks and time.

And an even greater challenge: knowing how to manage my relationship with the client. I didn't learn until later that beginning technical writers rarely begin as consultants. Fortunately, things worked out well—but it was clear I had a lot of work to do, because being a good writer was only part of being a competent technical writer.

My first permanent staff position came a short time later, and my career took off. I haven't looked back since. Through ups and downs in the economy, and working both as a consultant and a staff employee, I've seen the evolution of the field of technical writing from many different perspectives. I've learned a lot about what matters and what *not* to do.

I was lucky—I began my career at a time of explosive growth in the technology industry. But now, 20 years later, I can say with confidence that anybody with determination, curiosity, and good communication skills can be a technical writer.

I've lost count of how many times I've been asked "how do I become a technical writer?" You might say I wrote this book out of necessity, to help you avoid the pitfalls and surprises I encountered when starting my own career.

It won't be easy, but I promise it will be rewarding. What more could you ask for?

Why Become a Technical Writer?

Few jobs provide opportunities to work in almost any industry and geographic location, to constantly learn something new, and to be paid well for doing it. I don't know about you, but there are worse jobs than getting paid to be curious, to learn, and to help other people.

The Good

In 2010, US News and World Report named technical writing one of the "50 Best Careers" in the world. For me, the best part of being a technical writer is the variety of opportunities, but there are several practical benefits that I'd like to explain in detail.

Pay

Like any profession, compensation for technical writers fluctuates with economic realities. The median annual salary in 2011 for an experienced technical writer (2-3 years or more) was over $60,000 USD, and reached $80-$90K or more for senior positions in industries requiring specialized knowledge or experience. Even in difficult economic times, technical writers are usually well-compensated professionals.

In my own recent experience, starting salaries for technical writers with little or no experience in 2012 range from $35,000 to $50,000 per year, or about $20-$25 per hour. Starting salaries depend a great deal on the industry and your background, with the software and health care industries offering the highest starting salaries.

Opportunity

Technical writing opportunities exist in almost every industry, from banking to construction. Though many industries require some specialization of skills and processes, this means that—with a mastery of basic skills and a little experience—you can find a wide variety of opportunities.

One benefit for those just starting out: you can "try out" different industries and types of technical writing jobs to see what suits your interest and passions. Don't like software? Try health care. Not interested in banking? How about environmental science?

Mobility

Technical writers work all over the world, making a living in places from Iraq to Beijing, in small towns, large cities, and everywhere in between. Many technical writers telecommute as virtual workers. I've worked in an office and at home, and even "commuted" by plane between two parts of the country for a client.

In other words, being a technical writer means you're not limited to one type of workplace or geographic area. As you gain experience, it becomes easier to find technical writing work that allows you to work anywhere you've got an Internet connection and power. I once spent a week working from a cabin at the beach, with my feet propped up and the ocean outside my window. This isn't a fantasy— if you're skilled and willing to work hard, there are many opportunities like this for experienced technical writers.

The Bad

Technical writing isn't always rosy. Wherever you work, you'll likely encounter three challenges over and over again:

- **Project work**: Projects always have shifting schedules, priorities, and goals. Change will be the rule, not the exception.
- **Deadlines**: Work hours may be irregular as you strive to meet deadlines and project milestones—and deadlines often change.
- **Respect**: Most of the time, technical writers are respected professionals. But sometimes you'll struggle to receive the same respect and acknowledgement that engineers, scientists, and other technical staff do.

Do This

1. In 2-3 sentences, describe why you want to be a technical writer. Take your time and be thoughtful, refining it until it sounds like you. This is important, and will be useful as you progress through this book, build your resumé and conduct a job search.
2. Using *glassdoor.com*, *salary.com*, *payscale.com* and any other resources you can find (see the *Resources* section), determine the salary range in your geographic area (or the location you'd like to work in). If you're near a local chapter of the Society for Technical Communication (STC), see if they've created or shared any recent salary surveys (membership may be required to see this data).

What is Technical Writing?

I believe that "technical writing" *is not a specific kind of writing.*

That might sound strange, given the proliferation of books about technical writing, and the growing number of college degrees and certificates in technical writing. But though there are many *techniques* and *strategies* for communicating technical information, I have yet to find one universally agreed upon definition of what technical writing *is.*

Here's how I define technical writing:

The art of communicating a technical subject in a way that is understandable by and useful to a defined audience.

In other words, making the connection between a *technical subject*, an *audience*, and a specific *purpose*. Technical writing requires all three.

And notice I said "art", not "science". The key challenge in defining technical writing is that it is more of an approach than precise science. Though it's typically based on writing well—and there are many rules and guidelines for writing well—at its core, technical writing is nothing more than clearly communicating technical information for a specific purpose.

In everyday practice, technical writing is:

1. **Collaborative**: Few technical writers work alone. Most technical writing is a highly collaborative process—your work is reviewed and corrected by subject matter experts, co-designed with peers, and co-written with other technical writers or experts.
2. **Diverse**: From white papers to user guides for astronauts, there's rarely a topic or category of technical knowledge where technical writers aren't involved.
3. **Practical**: Technical writing is focused on real-world topics, problems and goals—how to perform a task, documenting science experiment results, understanding technical concepts.
4. **Audience-centered**: Good technical writing is tailored to a specific audience (or audiences), and made as clear and applicable as possible to the reader.

I've known many technical writers who made careers out of writing software manuals. Another wrote training materials for factory workers building printers. Yet another now helps scientists explain test procedures so other scientists can duplicate them. One of the best technical writers I know spends much of her day writing technical marketing materials for physicians and nurses.

Each of these writers follow different strategies and writing styles, use different tools, and write for very different audiences. But they all share the same goal: clearly communicating technical material in a way that is understandable and useful to their defined audience.

So what does this mean for you, just starting out in technical writing? It means you should focus on:

- Developing your communication skills and abilities
- Knowing the preferred styles, processes and tools of your chosen industry
- Basic techniques for understanding and writing for your audience.

Don't worry about learning to write "technically", because you'll be wasting your time. Instead, learn to write clearly and effectively, learn the basic tools to do that, and learn how to understand and communicate to your specific audience. For more advice on these three skills, see *Five Must-Have Skills*.

Do This

1. Write your own definition of technical writing, based on what you already know. Then, find at least five other definitions of technical writing and compare them to your own. What do they have in common? How are they different? Which ones sound appropriate to you?

2. Find three definitions of "audience analysis", and compare them. Based on your comparison, write a brief definition of audience analysis that makes sense to you—this basic understanding will come in handy in job interviews.

Life as a Technical Writer

For most technical writers, no two days on the job are exactly alike.

This doesn't mean you won't spend days, weeks, or months working on the same project, or encounter the same problems over and over again. What it means is that the popular image of a technical writer sitting at a computer and writing all day is a myth. There's so much more.

One of the most common complaints I hear from new technical writers is that they spend much of their time *not writing*. They interview subject matter experts, analyze audience needs, design and produce documents, manage projects and deadlines, attend meetings, perform research, and many other tasks.

If you're like me, you thrive on this kind of work style—it keeps things interesting and provides opportunities to learn and grow. In 20 years, I've yet to work on a project where there weren't surprises and unexpected challenges. Yet every time, I got real opportunities to solve problems and create something useful.

Where Do Technical Writers Work?

If there's an industry, technical writers probably work in it. Though technology fields like computer software are popular, you'll also find technical writers working in:

- Corporate operations
- Education
- Engineering

- Government
- Healthcare
- Manufacturing
- Military
- Sciences
- Computer hardware

And many more. Some of these (the military, for example) have explicit and detailed requirements for how a technical writer communicates information. As a technical writer, you'll be expected to learn and apply those requirements.

As you shape your strategy for becoming a technical writer, I recommend looking at these different areas and choosing one or two to focus on, because it will improve your chances of employment and future success. Later, with experience, you can branch out into different areas.

What Do Technical Writers Create?

Because it's closely tied to technology and science, the nature of technical writing changes to keep pace with the subject matter and the needs of the audience. For example, when I started my career, sets of printed manuals and floppy disks were the norm—but today, much of what I write is viewed in a web browser or an embedded help system.

Some technical writers still create those sets of manuals, while others never touch tools like Microsoft Word. Here is a (very) partial list of the kinds of communication you can expect to create:

- Audio/video content
- Illustrations, diagrams, mockups, flowcharts

- Instructions
- Journal articles
- Marketing materials
- Online help systems
- Policies and procedures
- Scientific papers
- Specifications
- Technical reports
- Training materials
- User guides
- Web content
- White papers

In my own career, I've created all of the above. But many technical writers I know are focused on two or three or these. So—don't try and learn how to create all of these now. Instead, focus on sharpening your communication skills and cultivating your ability to learn new tools and subjects.

Projects and Deadlines

A technical writer's work life is dictated by projects— working to deadlines, adapting to changing project goals and priorities, and working with limited time and resources. And often, working on more than one project at a time.

A project might last a few hours, a day, or two years, but there are always deadlines. If you're part of team that ships products (like software) or supports critical, time-sensitive outcomes (like satellite launches), being able to work to deadlines—and meet them—is what separates good technical writers from unemployed ones.

Why is this important? Because learning to think and operate in terms of projects and deadlines is mandatory if you're going to succeed as a technical writer. When I began to do this, and learned how to manage my time well and be flexible about change, I became a much more successful (and happier) technical writer.

Perceptions

Perceptions of technical writers are different in every industry and company. In some, technical writers are well-respected professionals working alongside engineers and scientists as peers; in others, they're "support" staff, considered more administrative than creative or technical. One engineer may respect your work and abilities; another may consider his profession the only "real" one at the company.

Short-term contract technical writers often work with a different perception. Typically hired to do what no staff writer was willing (or had time) to do, technical writers working on contract have both the freedom of working "outside" the culture of their client, and the constraint of being considered an outsider.

I've thrived in (and experienced) all of these environments. You can too, if you're willing to adapt. And remember: if you're just starting a career in technical writing, *any experience is good experience.*

Who You'll Work With

Technical writers often have a unique role in organizations. At any given time, you might:

- Interview engineers to better understand a technology or get information
- Discuss white papers with marketing staff
- Evaluate help system problems with quality assurance staff
- Prepare and distribute review drafts of your work
- Plan documentation projects with other technical writers
- Co-write with other technical writers.

And much more—often all on the same day. In other words, the technical writer often has a unique "generalist" role, because they routinely work with people across the organization, from scientists to marketers.

A Day In The Life of a Technical Writer

When I first started out in technical writing, I kept a daily journal of my experience to help me remember what was happening. Here's a "typical" day from my first years as a technical writer. I was working at a mid-sized software company.

Keep in mind this was before the advent of the Web's popularity, but little has changed in the intervening years. It's as typical a day as you'll find in the life of a technical writer. And yes—it was a real day.

8am: The day begins
I arrive at the office, turn on computer, and pour a cup of coffee. Today's going to be busy.

8:15am: E-mail and meeting prep

Coffee in hand, I read urgent messages and take a quick look at my calendar and master project schedule. I also gather up information for my 8:30 project meeting.

8:30am: Project "A" team meeting

The team for one of my two major projects meets every week at this time. We're still early in the project, so the mood is relaxed. When it's my turn, I give a quick review of my schedule and deadlines, reminding several people of an upcoming review. I also schedule time with two engineers to discuss the user interface of a new product.

9am: Writing time

I'm halfway through the last draft of a software user's guide that's due in three weeks, so I write as much as possible.

9:50am: Interview an engineer who suddenly has time

I've been trying to get an engineer to meet with me and describe product functionality. He shows up unannounced and is ready to discuss. We sit down and start going over my questions.

10am: Back to writing

The engineer suddenly remembered he had a 10am meeting to attend, but promises to return later to finish the interview. I return to writing the manual.

10:30am: Feedback review

I meet with two other technical writers to review feedback from a recent review of my latest draft. I've already summarized the feedback, so we spend the time discussing and prioritizing the most important issues.

11:15am: A quick review

A marketer asks me for a "quick review" of a white paper they're sending out to a potential customer at the end of the day. I've reviewed this document before, so I agree to a quick review before lunch.

12pm: "Lunch"

I brought my lunch, so (as I often do) I eat while working on Project "B". The next deadline is three weeks away, and there's too much to do before then.

1:30pm: Project "B" team meeting

The project "B" team is finally meeting today, after canceling the last two meetings. The project is in crisis, because we've missed the shipping deadline and customers are unhappy. As part of the compromise, we set a new aggressive deadline, and I revise the scope of what I'm expected to deliver—more, but in less time.

2:45pm: Reassess my schedule

I look at my own schedule and begin assessing how to juggle priorities in light of the new "Project B" schedule.

2:47pm: Troubleshooting with QA

A member of the QA team drops by to discuss a problem with how online help is displayed in a new product. We spend a lot of time tracking down the problem, but figure it out.

3:30pm: Continue reassessing my schedule

I return to reviewing my schedule and figuring out how to change a few deadlines to accommodate Project B.

4pm: Writing time
More writing of the user's guide. As I write, I start to see a need for an additional draft and review, but realize that the team won't have time. It's almost the end of the day; I'll reassess the project tomorrow.

4:55pm: Tracking down reviews
I go looking for two people who didn't return review copies, because I want to review all the feedback tonight in time for a meeting tomorrow.

5pm: Another quick review
No luck. The marketer stops me in the hallway to ask a few questions about the white paper. I scan the document and see spelling errors; I diplomatically suggest proofreading it before sending it out. They ask if I can do it.

5:30pm: Home to work
Proofreading complete and review copies in hand, I head home. I'll look them over before the next morning's meeting with my manager—I want to be prepared.

Alternative Titles for Technical Writers

Many people looking to break in to technical writing are surprised to find that "technical writers" have many different titles. Here are several (real world) examples of titles that I've seen (and held) in the past 20 years:

- Analyst
- Content Developer
- Documentation Specialist

- Information designer (or developer, architect or engineer)
- Knowledge Author
- Programmer/Writer
- Technical Author
- Technical communicator
- Usability/User Analyst

As you search for your first technical writing job, be aware of these (and other) titles, and include them in your search.

Do This

1. Choose two or three of the areas described in *Where Do Technical Writers Work?* above. Create a brief profile of the employers in those areas that appeal to you: where are they? What do they make? What do their job announcements for technical writers look like? Add this information to your technical writing notebook.
2. Identify 3-5 types of writing described in *What Do Technical Writers Create?* above. Do you have any writing samples already that fit into any of these categories? If not, could you create any?

Five Must-Have Skills

When looking at job descriptions for technical writers, you might be discouraged—how can you possibly have all those skills? Know all those software tools? Be well-versed in concepts like DITA, XML, CMS, and version control systems? Be a FrameMaker expert, an Illustrator expert, a Flare expert, and a Microsoft Word expert?

Relax. While you need *some* technical expertise, you don't have to be an expert to land your first technical writing job. And despite what you may have heard, **there is no universal set of tools for technical writers**. Knowing content creation tools is important, but those tools change all the time. What's popular in one industry is useless in another, or is replaced by a newer, better, faster tool.

Instead, focus on learning a few basic tools that are common in your chosen industry, and **be able to quickly learn new tools at any time**. That ability will give your career longevity, and in the long run, give you more career options.

Based on my experience as a technical writer, there are five essential skills you must have to start working successfully as a technical writer. They're not *all* you need to know but they're critical if you want to break into technical writing.

1: Communicate clearly and effectively

You've heard this already in earlier parts of this book. What does it mean? At the very least, you *must* be able to proofread, understand and use the active voice, and be able to revise and edit your own work (and the work of others).

How to acquire this skill

There is no "best" way to learn how to write and communicate well, but one thing is certain: you must have a solid understanding of the basic rules of written communication.

To do this, I always recommend two resources to every beginning technical writer. They're worth purchasing, because they can serve as reference and practice material for the rest of your professional life:

- Strunk & White's *Elements of Style*: About 95 pages long, you can read this book in an afternoon—but the clear, pithy explanations of how to write well are timeless.
- Wilson and Glazier's *The Least You Should Know About English*: Every good writer should be able to complete the exercises in this book. If you do, I promise you'll be a much stronger and better writer. I encountered this book several years into my own career, and it helped me with my own writing weaknesses.

Another excellent (and brief) resource is *Technical Writing Basics*, available as a free PDF at:

web.mit.edu/me-ugoffice/communication/
technical-writing.pdf

This is a good, high-level, easy to understand overview of technical writing basics, and matches my own real-world experience.

2: Create, modify, and produce documents

If you already have this skill—congratulations. If you want to be a technical writer, you must be *proficient* at it. At a minimum, you must be able to:

1. Create and produce documents in any size or orientation
2. Create, modify, and apply document templates and styles
3. Generate tables of contents and figures, and indexes
4. Create and modify headers, footers, and page numbers
5. Place, arrange, and scale graphics, charts, and tables
6. Create and manage revisions (most software now tracks multiple revisions via revision marks).

For some readers, this may seem like a basic list. They *are* basic for competent technical writers, so be sure you're able to do them.

How to acquire this skill

Don't be intimidated by this list: you can learn these tasks in a few days of focused learning. To keep it simple (and free), download and install either of the following:

- **OpenOffice**
  http://www.openoffice.org
- **Microsoft Office** (30 or 60-day trial version)
  http://office.microsoft.com/en-us/try/

If you don't have a computer, most public libraries and state employment offices provide access to word processing software (like Microsoft Word).

To learn the tasks listed above in OpenOffice, either visit the OpenOffice FAQ:

http://wiki.services.openoffice.org/wiki/
Documentation/FAQ)

You can also access instructions in the OpenOffice help system.

Microsoft offers free basic training for Microsoft Office here:

http://office.microsoft.com/en-us/
word-help/CH010369478.aspx

Also, you'll find hundreds of instructional videos on YouTube that teach you how to perform the six tasks listed above.

3: Know industry-specific terminology and styles

Every industry has its own vocabulary—terms, abbreviations, and acronyms. Many industries also have explicit ways of communicating information—document formats, formal language, and production processes. As a beginning technical writer, you'll be expected to know the basic terminology, styles, and communication methods of the industry you're aiming for.

For most industries, the *Chicago Manual of Style* or the *AP Stylebook* are the stylistic standard. Even if a potential employer doesn't use either of these, familiarity with them demonstrates that you're serious about writing well, and that you know common standards—and if a potential employer *does* use them, all the better.

How to acquire this skill

Access the *Chicago Manual of Style* or *AP Stylebook*. You can subscribe to and preview both of these online, or buy a print copy (though print copies are expensive). If you can afford it, purchase a copy or a subscription (or get one from the public library), and learn how they're organized and how to search them.

Also, take time to create (or find) a glossary of the common vocabulary and styles of the industry you're aiming for. See the *Glossary* section at the end of this book for a list of common technical writing terms. Writing out your own definitions will help you better understand and remember terminology.

Find 3-5 sample documents (or web pages, help files, or other writing examples) published by companies in the industry you're interested in. Look at how the terminology and information is presented.

If possible, find technical writers (or others) that work at these companies, and ask if they're willing to provide information about the vocabularies, style guides, and standards that they use. Most technical writers are willing to help, and you'll gain a few valuable contacts.

4: Understand the writing process

At its simplest, the writing process is writing and revising. But for a technical writer—who often collaborates with technical experts and other peers—the process is always more complex. It can involve:

- Planning and research
- Audience analysis
- (Multiple) reviews
- Editing and revising
- Approvals
- Formatting
- Production
- Delivery
- Document control

Depending on what you're writing, there could also be additional technical steps (for example, producing a help system for a software product or website). What's more, every workplace will do it differently. Even in the most casual environment, however, you'll be collaborating with others to develop drafts and produce work.

How to acquire this skill

Since the writing process varies so widely, it's difficult to "learn" a specific writing process outside the work environment. Try to learn as much as you can about the industry (or companies, if you know them) you're targeting. If possible, contact people who work in that industry. And to get a general overview of the writing process, I highly recommend Gerson's *Technical Writing: Process and Product* (5th Edition, but any edition will do).

5: Know how to ask questions

I've always spent a significant part of my workday as a technical writer interviewing people and doing research. These two activities are at the heart of the technical writing profession, and knowing how to ask the right questions and engage with subject matter experts and peers is what separates good technical writers from great ones.

In some ways, technical writers *depend* on experts and others to do their work—we both learn from them to write for an audience, and collaborate with them to shape what we write. Technical writing is rarely a solitary job—it's built on collaboration. This doesn't mean that you'll rely on others to tell you what (and how) to write, but you *will* rely on them for information, guidance, validation, and fact checking.

How to acquire this skill

This is a "people" skill that you'll mostly learn on the job, both by interacting with subject matter experts and watching other technical writers do it.

To develop your skills in asking questions and working with subject matter experts, I highly recommend an article from the STC's Technical Communication Journal titled *Technical Writer/Subject-matter Expert Interaction: The Writer's Perspective, the Organizational Challenge*, available at:

www.design4instruction.com/articles/pdf/
SME_TechWriter.pdf

It's a thoughtful, researched, real-world example of what it's like to work with subject matter experts. You can download it for free from the link above, or purchase it from the STC or on Amazon.

Do This

1. Read Strunk & White's *Elements of Style* and Wilson and Glazier's *The Least You Should Know About English*.
2. Download and install OpenOffice or Microsoft Office, and practice the six tasks described in the chapter until you become proficient at them.
3. Access the *Chicago Manual of Style* and *AP Stylebook*, and learn how they're organized and how to search for information.
4. Create (or find) a glossary of the common vocabulary and styles of the industry (or industries) you're interested in.
5. Find and evaluate 3-5 sample documents (or web pages, help files, or other writing examples) published by companies in the industry you're interested in. Take note of terminology, style, acronyms, language, and format.
6. Read Gerson's *Technical Writing: Process and Product*, focusing on the sections that describe project management and the writing process.
7. Read *Technical Writer/Subject-matter Expert Interaction: The Writer's Perspective, the Organizational Challenge* (see link above).

Should I Get More Education or Training?

The short answer: probably not.

I'll make it even simpler than that—if you already have a bachelor's degree and want to get into technical writing quickly, **don't pursue another degree or training program now.**

In other words: *skills and experience are what matter most.* Education or training are icing on the cake when you're trying to get your foot in the door.

But—if you *don't* have a bachelor's degree (in any subject), you'll have a difficult time competing for technical writing positions. If that's the case for you, consider obtaining a four-year degree before launching your career. While in college, you can aggressively pursue internships along the way (see *How Do I Get Experience?* for more information).

Job descriptions are *ideals*

Despite the job descriptions you read and common beliefs about college, most employers of technical writers don't care what degree you have, or whether you've progressed beyond the baccalaureate level. Job descriptions are *ideals*, and are often written by human resources staff (who aren't technical writers) using a template. For more information about how employers read resumés, see *How Do I Get Hired?*

Don't Worry about College Majors

Some employers advertise for people with a technical degree (computer science, engineering, or a science discipline), but if you don't have one of these—and you're looking to get into technical writing as quickly as possible—don't worry.

Though there's nothing wrong with a technical degree, the best technical writers I've known had a broad-based education rather than a specialized one. I have an undergraduate degree in History, and I've hired (or helped hire) about two dozen technical writers in my own career. Not one hiring decision was made based on what college degree the candidate had (other than whether or not they had at least a four-year degree). Only one had a degree in technical communication, and two others had technical degrees. The rest held degrees in everything from English to Psychology.

What About Two-Year Degrees?

Whether or not you already have a college degree, I recommend avoiding community college training in "technical writing". It won't impress many employers, and the training is often so basic that it's not useful. In the past 20 years, I've only worked with one technical writer who had community college training in technical communication—and they regretted it.

What About Training and Certifications?

Training and certification matters most when you are developing and advancing your technical writing career, not when you're just starting out. After you've got your first job, you'll have a much better idea of how (and if) more education or training can benefit your career. So for now— I recommend waiting to pursue training and certifications.

But: if you don't have *any* training or experience in communication or basic skills in software tools, you may benefit from a course or other short-duration, focused training experience.

This kind of training doesn't have to cost anything or take a lot of time, if you're resourceful and learn quickly; there are thousands of free written, audio, and video resources on the Web and at your local public library.

Some of the kinds of training you might look for are:

- **Project management practices**: Agile, Lean, PMP certification
- **Content creation tools**: Microsoft Office, Visio, and Project, Adobe FrameMaker, Captivate, RoboHelp, InDesign, and Photoshop, LaTeX, OpenOffice
- **Content management systems**: Microsoft SharePoint, Joomla, Plone, Drupal, wikis
- **Web technologies**: XML, HTML, CSS, PHP, databases

The key concept here is *focused*: the kind of training that will really help you prepare for and land a job are the complementary skills to communication like project management, technology skills, document production, and specialized skills pertaining to the area or industry you're interested in joining.

See *Five Must-Have Skills* and the *Resources* section at the end of the book for specific resources I've found useful in learning and growing my skills.

Do This

1. Find 10 working technical writers on LinkedIn.com, and note their educational background and other formal training. How many have degrees in technical communication? Do any have professional certifications? What patterns do you see?
2. For those same 10 writers, note their skills. What do they have in common? How many of these skills can you already put on your resumé?
3. Based on your research and this book, identify five skills that you want to acquire or improve, and one or two resources for each. Schedule time to take your skill to the next level, and set a goal (a week, a month, a year). *Put these skills on your resumé.*

How Do I Get Experience?

If you're reading this book, "how do I get experience?" might be your most urgent question. I know—I've seen and written job postings, and I've also experienced the frustration and discouragement of reading them.

It's true—employers typically prefer to hire people with relevant experience. They look for specific skills and clear examples of you doing work that's similar to what they'll hire you to do.

But don't be discouraged. People get their first technical writing jobs every day, and you can be one of them. If you have little (or no) experience, then you can create it—fast—by focusing on what employers need.

There are five actions that I've seen work repeatedly for people starting out in technical writing:

1. **Leverage what you already have**
2. **Volunteer**
3. **Get (or create) an internship**
4. **Create samples**
5. **Create a portfolio**

Each of these actions is important—if you want to get hired, I strongly suggest doing *all* of them.

1: Leverage What You Already Have

All of your writing experience counts. This doesn't mean employers want to see that short story you wrote in high school, but short, polished examples of writing that show your communication skills are fair game. The goal is to demonstrate your ability to clearly communicate complex ideas and technical subjects.

This might be a 2-3 page example from a manual, a web page, a short "how-to" video, or something else—ideally on a technical subject. Gather the examples you have, and pick the very best of them to polish and put in your portfolio (see #5 below).

But communication experience is only part of what you'll need. Have you solved technical problems? Managed a project of any size? Attended workshops, training, or seminars? These count, and the best ones should be on your resumé.

2: Volunteer

Several open source software projects (see the *Resources* section) are constantly looking for help creating software documentation and instructions. Pick one and join up— **find one small area where you can contribute, and go for it**. Start small, and keep looking for ways to do more.

As soon as you have created something, *save it in your portfolio*. Voilà—it becomes part of your experience. I can't tell you how many technical writers I've known who got their start this way.

Nonprofits are also a rich source of opportunities, and are always looking for help—for free, if possible. A brief search of your area will likely turn up several who are eager for your help. Volunteer to write training materials, short "how to" guides, policies—anything that can help demonstrate your communication skills.

And wherever you volunteer your skills, when you're done, *ask for recommendations.* These experiences and contacts are valuable, and help build the story of your experience. they also show that you're serious about technical writing.

3: Get (or Create) an Internship

Don't be shy—if you can't find an established internship, go out and create your own. After you've found companies or organizations that you're interested in, create a concise explanation of the kind of experience you're looking for, and include your goals. Make this part of a 1-2 page internship proposal, and make sure it includes how the internship will benefit the company.

Contact the organizations, and ask for opportunities to share or present your internship proposal. Don't give up— follow up until you've got an internship. Believe me—it works.

4: Create Samples

Don't have any samples? Create some. Remember, the goal is not to demonstrate how much you know about technology or a particular subject, but that you know how to format a document and write clear, understandable instructions and explanations.

Here are a few ideas that I've seen work well for new writers:

1. Choose any subject and write a 10-15 page how-to guide for it that includes a cover page, table of contents, index, and glossary.
2. Create several 1-2 page "cheat sheets" that help users perform a specific task (or tasks)—for example, how to set up a basic book template in Microsoft Word. Use graphics and layout to make it visually appealing, and make sure it's *accurate*. It doesn't matter if this has been done before by others—the goal is to present *your* work and style.
3. Create a "how to" video on a subject that interests you. You can present this on YouTube or another website.
4. Rewrite instructions from popular software products. Be careful here—don't plagiarize, but instead make it your own.
5. Pick a complex technical or scientific topic and using visual aids, explain it in a clear and engaging way. For example, I know of one technical writer who got hired based on her 10-page explanation (with images) of how astronauts prepare for space shuttle missions on launch day.

5: Create a Portfolio

Most technical writers keep portfolios of their work—tangible examples of their best work.

If you want to break into technical writing, a portfolio is crucial for two reasons: it shows employers that's you're serious about becoming a technical writer, and it demonstrates your skills and experiences.

Don't be intimidated by the term "portfolio", though. It can be as simple as printed pages, but could include web links, videos, an online help system, or even a web site that shows off examples of your work. It can be electronic or printed, a collection of samples or a flashy website—or a combination of all of these. Over time, you'll add (and remove) samples as you collect experience and target different employers.

There is no one best way to create a portfolio. The key is to have samples ready for potential employers, and that the portfolio contents look professional—that is, the examples should be your best work, and as polished and sharp as possible.

My own portfolio has evolved over time. Today, it's an electronic presentation of several samples, each including a brief story about the associated project—what it entailed, what I learned, what skills and experience I applied to (and gained from) it. Every employer I've shown this loves it, because it gives context and a more complete story to what I've done. It shows my experience *and* my skills *and* tells a story.

And here's another idea: after you've put together your portfolio, find people in the industry who will critique it. Be honest about where you are—a person who's creating their portfolio for the first time and looking to break in. Be ready to accept tough criticism, and then use it to make your portfolio better.

Do This

1. Identify three open source software projects or local nonprofits that need technical writing help. Contact all three and explain that you're looking for opportunities to build your portfolio. If you find a suitable project, go for it. If not, identify three more project or nonprofits and do it again.
2. If you prefer to get an internship, find 2 or 3 organizations that you're interested in, and craft a 1-2 page internship proposal using the guidelines in #3 above.
3. Gather your very best writing samples. If it's of good enough quality, polish it and add it to your portfolio (excerpting portions, if necessary). Don't worry about creating a website or other electronic version yet—just gather electronic files or other materials into a central place, and call it your portfolio. This is only the first step.
4. Create a portfolio. Remember, for now this only has to be polished examples of your work that you can send (and show) to potential employers upon request.

How Do I Get Hired?

Getting hired as a technical writer is no more (or less) difficult than getting other professional jobs. To have the best chance of success, you've got to be prepared, persistent, and focused; leave out one or two of those three things, and the rest won't matter.

Remember—when hiring, employers have only three questions in mind:

1. **Experience**
    Have you done enough of this work before? (See *How Do I Get Experience?*)
2. **Skills**
    Do you have the skills and abilities to do this job? (See *How Do I Get Experience?*, *Five Must-Have Skills*, and *Do I Need More Education or Training?*)
3. **Fit**
    Does your personality and style fit well with the rest of the team?

The first two are within your control, but #3 is not. You'll need to decide if the employer is a good fit for *you*, however; most job seekers forget that how a workplace fits them is as important as how they fit the workplace.

There are five points I focus on when seeking work or hiring others. I believe they apply to any career and level of experience, but especially to people with little or no experience:

1. Think like an employer
2. Be a solution to a problem

3. Have the essential skills
4. Promote yourself
5. Be committed, but flexible.

Each of these are explained below.

1: Think like an employer

"Think like an employer" means setting aside your own goals and needs for a moment and sitting in the employer's chair.

Employers aren't thinking about *your* goals and needs—they're thinking about *theirs*. Think about that. When you apply for a position or arrive for an interview, employers expect you to help them understand who you are—and how you can help them meet their goals and needs. The three things I mentioned above—experience, skills, and fit—are what they're thinking about.

As you think like an employer, try and answer these questions about potential employers:

- What do they do?
- What problems do they have?
- What do they expect of employees?
- What are their most important goals and needs?
- What kind of people work there, and what is their reputation?

Then, look at every aspect of yourself—your resumé, skills, experience, attitude, appearance, approach, personality. How might they appear to an employer?

Early in my career, another technical writer and I would practice interviews by taking turns being the employer. We asked the most direct and difficult questions we could think of: why should I hire you and not another candidate? What do you know about my company? Why do you want to work here and not at Company X? Can you help me solve my problems? It helped prepare me for almost anything, and shook me out of my "me"-focused approach to job hunting. If you can, find someone and do this exercise—I guarantee it will make you a better candidate.

2: Be a Solution to a Problem

This is the essence of any career, but I've found it to be especially true in technical writing careers. When an employer seeks to hire someone, it's because they've got a problem to solve: not enough staff to complete projects, a good (or bad) employee left, their operations are expanding.

It's crucial that you find out what the employer's chief problem is. For example, an employer might see their problem this way: "Customers complain about our manuals all the time—that they're too long, or too hard to read. This is beginning to cost us business. We need a new technical writer who can write outstanding manuals that customers rave about."

Listen carefully to the employer to discern their problems. Whatever the problem, it's up to you to (a) find out what it is, and (b) explain how and why you're part of the solution. If you're not part of the solution to a problem, why would any employer hire you?

3: Have the Essential Skills

See *Five Must-Have Skills* above. Make sure you have (or acquire) the skills and abilities an employer is looking for, *and* that you can explain how you'll use those skills and abilities to help solve their problem.

Even better, target employers and organizations that are looking for the skills and abilities *you already have*. In other words, instead of trying to fit yourself into the job descriptions you find, first look for employers that are looking specifically for people like you.

4: Promote Yourself.

If you're like me, self-promotion is difficult. But if you want to break in to technical writing, you'll have to get over any fear of introducing yourself and asking for help. Here are four basic steps you can take now to get started:

1. **Get a business card**: Get simple, easy-to-read business cards with your name, e-mail address, phone number, title, and LinkedIn.com profile address (see #2). For "title", put "technical writer". Don't be shy—employers don't hire those that want to *become* technical writers—they hire those that *are*.
2. **Create a LinkedIn.com profile**: Create a polished, professional profile on LinkedIn.com, and start connecting to people who can help you in your search. While you're there, join groups that interest you and participate in (and start) discussions.

3. **Get an "elevator speech"**: Having a concise, 1-3 sentence statement that describes who you are and what you have to offer can be a powerful tool. For example: "*I'm a self-directed communications expert with current skills in online help development and health care practices. I love helping customers and users succeed with technology.*" Put this at the top of your resumé, on the back of your business card, and on your LinkedIn profile, and repeat it to potential employers and others who might appreciate knowing about you.

4. **Join professional organizations**: If you can afford it, consider joining the STC as soon as possible. Meanwhile, seek out the nearest chapter and begin attending events and workshops. This will help you meet fellow technical writers, start making connections, and learn the local business environment. See the *Resources* section for links to other organizations.

5: Be Committed, But Flexible

Be willing to take on tasks and opportunities that aren't your first choice. Research different geographic areas and less than ideal opportunities. For example, you might need to start working in finance to gain experience before you can work in health care, or write product descriptions and marketing materials when you'd rather be writing software manuals and environmental reports.

Job hunting can be emotionally draining. I know: I've been there many times. But I can say one thing with complete confidence: persistence is what makes the difference. *Don't give up*. And, learning to land your first technical writing job will make you better prepared for future job hunts. You'll be a smarter, sharper, more polished and prepared candidate with each job interview.

Everything You Need To Know About Resumés

You've probably seen and heard a lot of advice about resumés, and I'll bet most of it focused on how the resumé should *look*. I've got some bad news: how a resumé looks doesn't matter much anymore.

Why? Because most businesses (even smaller ones) now use software and databases to store and search resumés. This means that once you apply, special software (or sometimes, a human) searches applicant resumés for keywords and phrases, and sorts them accordingly. Some interviewers never see your actual formatted resumé.

Don't get me wrong. A neat, organized, error-free resumé is important—but how it looks (fonts, layout, headings, etc.) is rarely a deciding factor when choosing interviewees, whether or not it's a human process. What matters most is keywords and phrases.

But let's get one thing clear:

Resumés have only one purpose—to get you an interview.

After that, they're not too important. Resumés are a sales pitch, your strongest, best, and most concise way of telling employers that you can do the job, and why.

With that in mind, here are four key principles that will increase the chance that your resumé gets noticed:

1. **Keep it short** (3 pages or less): Longer resumés are never better, regardless of how much experience you have.
2. **Make it "search friendly"**: Include what you believe are the keywords from the job description (for example, skills).
3. **Make it error-free**: You're a technical writer. An error on your resumé means a lot more than someone who doesn't write for a living, so be sure there aren't any.
4. **Keep it simple**: Use one or two fonts, a simple layout, and short, concise sentences in the active voice.

What to put on your resumé

There's no "best" way to organize or present a resumé. I put the most relevant information first, and always prefer to see resumés from applicants who do the same. I also customize my resumé for every employer, to ensure it matches up well to the language of the job announcement.

Here's a common way to organize sections of a resumé, and I recommend it for beginning technical writers. In order, from top to bottom:

- **Name, address, contact information**: Include your LinkedIn.com URL or professional website (if you have one).
- **Summary**: A brief (2-3 sentence) statement about who you are, what you have to offer, and what you're looking for. See "elevator speech" above.

- **Skills**: Be sure that these match the language of the job announcement. this includes software skills and other tools, but also complementary skills like project management and other organizational and interpersonal skills.
- **Experience**: Emphasize your title, employer name, and duties; de-emphasize dates.
- **Education**: Most relevant education first. If it seems appropriate, omit part (or all) of your education.
- **Professional memberships, affiliations, awards**: Keep this short, and make sure it's relevant to the position you're applying for.

No hobbies, jokes, quotations, references, graphics (unless it's a professional quality head photo of you)—just the list above.

How to Interview

To many people—even highly experienced ones—job interviews are a mysterious and anxious process. I've been there: do they like me? Did I give a stupid answer? Should I ask more questions?

Think of job interviews as conversations. The employer is interested in your experience, skills, and how well you might fit in, and you're interested in the details of the work, presenting yourself, and finding out if you might fit in.

In other words, job interviews are much more than a sales pitch and getting approval—they're really opportunities for you and the employer to get to know each other and talk about what matters to each of you. You should come prepared to ask questions, evaluate and get to know the employer, present yourself, and to listen.

Is that difficult when you're eager to get the job? Yes. But if you begin to see job interviews this way—as focused conversations—you'll be more in charge of your own career, a more attractive candidate, and ultimately happier in the jobs you do get.

Below, I've listed the essential steps you should take before, during, and after the interview. If it helps, print the steps out and use them as a checklist.

Before the interview

1. Think like an employer (see above).
2. Try and identify the employer's problems. How can you apply yourself and what you have to that problem?
3. Prepare portfolio samples, and be prepared to share and explain them.
4. Prepare at leave five questions that you want to ask the interviewer(s).
5. If possible, find out who will interview you.
6. Prepare references, and be prepared to share them at the interview.

During the interview

Remember, you are also interviewing the employer to learn as much as you can about them: is it a good fit for you? Is the job description accurate?

1. Attitude is *everything*. Smile. Be positive. Relax. Don't sit back and cross your arms or legs—sit forward and make eye contact.
2. Emphasize what you are willing to do to be better. You want to learn and grow, and employers want to know your goals and intentions.
3. If possible, collect a business card from everyone you speak to.
4. Ask questions: Focused questions help you understand the position better, and show employers you're interested and have done your homework.
5. Find out the employer's hiring timeline—will there be future interviews? Do they need references?

After the interview

1. Send thank you messages to every person you spoke to. Express gratitude for their time and attention. Reiterate what you've got to offer, and relate it to the company's problems and needs. And if you want the job, always ask for it in the message.

2. After a reasonable amount of time, follow up with a brief note to express your continued interest. Let them know that you'll follow up again, and when.

Contract, or Permanent Employment?

Your best bet? Permanent employment.

Most technical writers don't begin their careers as contract employees for one simple reason: employers want consultants who are experienced professionals with (often very) specific skills. They want a short-term problem solved, a product shipped, or to temporarily fill a suddenly vacant position. Large companies often hire contract employees for these (and accounting and liability) reasons. Large companies achieve a more flexible workforce by hiring contract employees.

If you're trying to break in to technical writing, you'll usually be at a strong disadvantage when applying for contract/consultant positions. It's a great opportunity, but evaluate contract opportunities carefully—you might be wasting your time until you've got more experience.

Finding Jobs and Employers

It's rare to find a job these days that isn't posted somewhere on the Internet. Though not all entry level jobs are posted online, most employers (of any size) now automatically post job announcements to sites like Indeed.com, LinkedIn.com, Dice.com, craigslist.org, and their own corporate website. Because of this practice, you'll find a lot of "cross-posting"—the same job appearing on several websites. For better or worse, there are only two meaningful ways that you'll get a job—by strategically searching and (and posting on) these kinds of websites, and by networking to become known to (and learn from) people that can help you find out about unposted positions and connect you to decision makers.

As a beginning technical writer, you need both: strategic searching, and intelligent networking.

Searching online

Searching sites like Indeed.com is straightforward—select search terms and sort the results. As you begin your job search, focus on these four strategies:

1. Look for job titles other than "technical writer" (see *Life as a Technical Writer* above).
2. Don't filter out jobs by experience level—instead, take time to read job descriptions of all levels to learn the different kinds of skills and experience that employers are looking for, and to preview the opportunities that await you after acquiring a few years of experience.
3. Post your resumé on craigslist.com, LinkedIn.com, Indeed.com, and any other site that serves the industry you're interested in (right now, you'll have the best results with the first three.) These don't have to be comprehensive, but should at least highlight your skills, experience, and goals.
4. Make a list of the top 10 companies that you'd like to work for, and search their job postings. Sign up to receive notifications about new positions, if possible. Then, visit LinkedIn.com and look at the profiles of employees (ideally, technical writers) that work at those companies. If it seems appropriate, contact them to ask for a connection and for advice on landing a job with their company.

Networking

As you might have guessed by now, I'm a big fan of
LinkedIn.com. Used well, it's one of the most powerful
career tools you have. It's not a "social" site like Facebook,
and you'll find thousands of other technical writers and
industry professionals there that can help you with
questions, suggestions, and introductions. Start with this
tool, and take time to become familiar with its capabilities.
Search LinkedIn groups and find one or two that appeal to
you, join them, and start reading and responding to posts.

Also, start participating in at least one professional
organization, like the STC. If you can afford it, become a
member; if not, start by finding a local chapter, attending
events and workshops, and introducing yourself to those
you meet. If you're serious about breaking in to technical
writing, getting involved with peers will help you find out
what's happening in the profession and local and regional
industries.

Do This

1. Using the guidelines in this chapter, create a
   resumé.
2. Create a LinkedIn.com profile. If you already have
   one, then be sure that it's complete and clearly
   communicates the skills and goals you have.
3. Create and print your business card and elevator
   speech. Who are you? What do you have to offer?
   What problem(s) do you solve?
4. Post your resumé to Indeed.com, craigslist.org, and
   Dice.com.

5. Make a list of the top 10 companies you'd like to work for, and learn as much as possible about them. What problems do they have? Who are their customers? What audience do they serve? Who works there? (See LinkedIn).
6. Sign up to receive notifications about new positions from those 10 companies. Then, visit LinkedIn.com and look at the profiles of employees (ideally, technical writers) that work at those companies. If it seems appropriate, contact them to ask for a connection and for advice on landing a job with their company.
7. Join or get involved in at least one professional organization, like the STC. Learn what resources they offer, and start meeting peers in your area that can help you learn about the profession and local/regional conditions.

Putting it All Together

In many ways, technical writing is an unusual profession. It requires the endless curiosity of a beginner, the spirit of a generalist, the "big picture" grasp of a CEO, the attention to detail of an engineer or scientist, a strong ability to learn and adapt—and more often than not, a thick skin.

It's a difficult profession to fully prepare for in advance. Beyond the skills and strategies I've described in this book, much of technical writing is learned on the job, through daily experience, training, and interaction with others.

Given that, it's challenging to describe a specific "plan", degree, or program that will guarantee you success and adequately prepare you for the work. There are practical strategies, but no magic formula. But if I've done my job, you should now have an idea of what its like to be a technical writer, and a set of basic tools and strategies that can help you become one.

Everything I've said here is based on my own 20 years of experience and the strategies I've seen work repeatedly. Other technical writers will have different stories and advice. If you become a technical writer, you'll have your stories, too.

If you haven't already, be sure to complete all of the tasks at the end of each chapter. Talk to working technical writers, and build your connections to the profession and the industries you're interested in. Consider keeping a journal of what you learn and what you've done—I did it for several years, and it was invaluable.

Remember—the key ingredient is *you*. Put in the time and effort to prepare yourself, get skills, network, go to interviews, overcome failure and obstacles, learn, and keep trying. New technical writers get their first job every day; you can become one of them, if you want to bad enough. I hope you'll go for it.

Resources

Career Research

Glassdoor.com
http://www.glassdoor.com/index.htm

Money: 100 Best Companies to Work For in 2011
http://money.cnn.com/magazines/fortune/
bestcompanies/2011/snapshots/1.html

Payscale.com
http://www.payscale.com

Salary.com
http://www.salary.com

U.S. News and World Report: Technical writing one of the "50 Best Careers" in 2011
http://money.usnews.com/money/careers/articles/2010/
12/06/best-careers-2011-technical-writer

The 25 Best Tech Companies to Work For
http://www.businessinsider.com/the-25-best-tech-
companies-to-work-for-2010-7

Job Search

Computerjobs.com
http://www.computerjobs.com/

Craigslist (search by city)
http://www.craigslist.org

Dice.com
http://www.dice.com

Indeed.com
http://www.indeed.com

LinkedIn
http://www.linkedin.com

Simplyhired.com
www.simplyhired.com

Learning

Adobe learning resources (most are free)
http://www.adobe.com/training/resources/

HTML Writers Guild
http://www.hwg.org/

Microsoft Word help and how-to
http://office.microsoft.com/en-us/word-help/

OpenOffice tutorials
http://wiki.services.openoffice.org/wiki/Documentation/
Tutorials

Webmonkey tutorials
http://www.webmonkey.com/tutorials/

W3C HTML tutorial
http://www.w3schools.com/html/html_intro.asp

W3C XML tutorial
http://www.w3schools.com/xml/xml_whatis.asp

YouTube
http://www.youtube.com

5-Minute DITA Tutorial
http://dita.xml.org/resource/5-minute-dita-tutorial

Professional Organizations

Association for Computing Machinery
http://www.acm.org/

American Medical Writers Association
http://www.amwa.org/

American Society of Business Publication Editors
http://www.asbpe.org/

American Society of Journalists and Authors
http://www.asja.org/

IEEE Professional Communication Society
http://ewh.ieee.org/soc/pcs/

International Association of Business Communicators
http://www.iabc.com/

Society for Technical Communication
http://www.stc.org/

Council of Science Editors
http://www.councilscienceeditors.org

HTML Writers Guild
http://www.hwg.org/

Institute of Scientific and Technical Communicators
http://www.istc.org.uk/

National Writers Union
http://www.nwu.org/

Women in Technology International
http://www.witi.com/

Resumés

Slideshare
http://www.slideshare.com

Top 5 Tips For Creating Impressive Video resumés
http://mashable.com/2011/01/17/tips-video-resumes/

How to Optimize Your LinkedIn Profile
http://mashable.com/2010/12/15/optimize-linkedin-profile/

Technical writer resumés on Indeed.com
http://www.indeed.com/resumes#!q=technical+writer

Software Tools

Adobe's Technical Communication Suite (free trial available)
http://www.adobe.com/products/technicalcommunication
suite/try.html

Author-it
http://www.author-it.com/

Camtasia
http://www.techsmith.com/camtasia.html

Captivate
http://www.adobe.com/products/captivate.html

FrameMaker
http://www.adobe.com/products/framemaker.html

Gimp
http://www.gimp.org/

HelpIQ
http://www.helpiq.com/

HelpLogic
http://www.ebutterfly.com/helplogic/

HelpScribble
http://www.helpscribble.com/

Madcap Software
http://www.madcapsoftware.com/

Omnigraffle
http://www.omnigroup.com/products/omnigraffle/

Photoshop
http://www.photoshop.com/products/photoshop

RoboHelp
http://www.adobe.com/products/robohelp.html

Snagit
http://www.techsmith.com/snagit.html

Visio
http://visio.microsoft.com

Style Guides and Standards

ACM SIGDOC
http://www.sigdoc.org/

APA Style
http://www.apastyle.org/

The Associated Press Stylebook
http://www.apstylebook.com/

The Chicago Manual of Style
http://www.chicagomanualofstyle.org/home.html

Council of Science Editors
http://www.councilscienceeditors.org

Volunteer Technical Writing Opportunities

The Free Software Foundation
http://www.fsf.org/campaigns/gnu-press/authors

Apache OpenOffice.org
http://incubator.apache.org/openofficeorg/get-involved.html

OpenHatch
https://openhatch.org/

Ubuntu Documentation Team
https://wiki.ubuntu.com/DocumentationTeam

Mozilla
http://www.mozilla.org/contribute/areas.html
https://developer.mozilla.org/Project:en/How_to_Help

Gnome
http://www.gnome.org/get-involved/

Glossary

ACM
Association for Computing Machinery, a professional society for the profession and science of computing. The ACM has several subgroups (see SIGDOC below).

Active voice
A way of writing in which the subject is active (acts upon the verb) (e.g., *the man ate the hot dog*, where the subject (man) performs the verb (ate)). Contrast with passive voice, where the subject is passive (acted upon by the verb) (e.g., *the hot dog was eaten by the man*).

Agile
A project management approach, typically used in a software development environment. Agile focuses on small, iterative steps rather than linear, sequential steps.

AP Stylebook
A popular style of standard English usage in written communication. Produced by the Associated Press.

American Psychological Association (APA)
A professional organization that also produces a popular usage standard for English communication. APA style is commonly used both in academic and professional settings.

API
Application Programming Interface. A set of specifications for a software product that provide a way for other software to interact with it (an "interface").

Audience analysis
The process of identifying the needs and requirements of the users (or readers) of a product. Also called *needs analysis* or *user analysis*. Several formalized processes exist for analyzing audience needs.

Council of Science Editors (CSE)
A professional organization for organizing scientific communication practices and educating those writing in the sciences.

Chicago Manual of Style (CMS)
The CMS is a worldwide standard of standard English usage in written communication. Currently in its 16th edition, the CMS is also available online.

Chunking
A loosely defined method of breaking large amounts into smaller "chunks" (like lists and short sentences), using cues (like bold text, or graphics) to guide the reader's eye.

Content Management System (CMS)
A software tool (or collection of tools) that provide a way to systematically store and retrieve pieces of content like web pages, documents, and graphics. CMSes typically consist of a database component and a user interface component for managing the storage and retrieval of content. Microsoft SharePoint, WordPress, Joomla, and Drupal are examples of popular CMSes.

Cascading Style Sheet (CSS)
A language and format for defining how elements of markup languages (like HTML) are displayed in a web page or document. Most web pages use CSS to define the visual presentation of web pages.

Cross-platform
A way of describing software or hardware that works on more than one type of computer and operating system.

Courseware
Educational material packaged for use with a computer. Courseware can be web-based, a standalone software package, or a combination of printed and electronic materials.

Datasheet
A document that summarizes the technical characteristics and functions of a tool or product (typically a physical one). Datasheets do not follow a standard format.

DITA
Darwin Information Typing Architecture. An XML-based set of rules and principles for authoring, producing, and delivering content.

Documentation
In technical writing, *documentation* commonly refers to user support materials like manuals and guides. Though used in several industries, this term is most commonly used in software product development.

Documentation plan

A document that typically describes the goals, intentions, design, and purpose of a documentation set or other technical writing product. Though common, documentation plans do not follow a standard format.

E-Learning

A general term used to describe any kind of instructional content presented in electronic form (for example, a web site).

End-user

The primary user of a product, typically a consumer.

FAQ

Frequently Asked Questions. A selected group of questions and answers intended to address the most popular and important questions asked by users, customers, or readers.

FrameMaker

A page layout and production software program made by Adobe Systems, Inc. A long-time industry standard for writing long (book-length) or complex printed documentation, and for "single-sourcing" technical writing products for different delivery methods (print, online, etc.)

GUI

Graphical User Interface. Though still used in the software and hardware industry, most computer interfaces are graphical; so, the more common term today is *user interface* or *interface.*

Help authoring tool (HAT)

A software product used to develop and deliver help content, typically for an embedded or standalone help system. Flare, RoboHelp, and Author-it are popular HATs.

InDesign

A document design and production tool produced by Adobe Systems, Inc. InDesign focuses on visual layout of documents, but also includes most of the textual features (page number, headers, sections) of tools like Microsoft Word.

Information Mapping

A structured, analytical (and proprietary) method for organizing and presenting information. Information Mapping uses an explicit system of structuring and labeling units of information to meet the needs of a defined audience.

Information architecture (IA)

Originally used as a general term for how information is organized, IA now typically refers to the structured organization and presentation of content, especially web sites.

Instructional design

A systematic and theory-based methodology for creating and presenting instructional materials.

Flare

A help authoring tool (HAT) produced by Madcap Software.

LaTeX

A markup language (like XML) used to prepare documents for high-quality typesetting. LaTeX is normally used with the TeX typesetting program, and is very popular in academia and scientific environments.

Localization

The process of adapting a product (typically software) for a particular language and culture. Also called *L10n* (the "10" referring to the number of letters between the first and last letters of "localization").

Milestone

An important date or moment in a project or process (e.g., a deadline, or when certain product features are complete).

OS X

"Operating System Ten", the current operating system for Apple's Macintosh computer. OS X is based in part on FreeBSD and NetBSD, two Unix-like operating systems.

Windows

Microsoft Windows, the operating system produced by Microsoft for a variety of personal computers (typically referred to as "PCs", though the Macintosh and others are also PCs).

Linux

An open-source, Unix-like operating system for PCs created by (and named for) Linus Torvalds.

Marcom

Common abbreviation for *marketing communication.*

Microsoft Office

A suite of software tools produced by Microsoft Corporation. The most inexpensive versions of Microsoft Office currently consist of Word, Excel, OneNote, and PowerPoint, but more expensive versions have additional tools.

Microsoft SharePoint

A web application and content management platform produced by Microsoft Corporation. Though SharePoint provides a host of application tools, it is most commonly used for content management and corporate intranet functions.

MLA

Modern Language Association. MLA-defined style is commonly used in academic settings (especially the humanities). MLA style is almost never used for technical writing.

Online help

Topical or instructional assistance provided to software users. Commonly used to refer to help systems (embedded or otherwise) that are part of a software product, online help can also refer generally to any type of help that is structured to help a user.

OpenOffice

A free, open source software application suite produced and managed by the Apache Software Foundation. OpenOffice features are similar to (and largely compatible with) Microsoft Office. OpenOffice includes word processing, spreadsheet, drawing, slide presentation and database programs.

Open source
A method and philosophy of producing and sharing software. Open source software typically provides public access to most or all parts of the product, and allows users to freely modify (but not sell) it. However, many companies produce products based on open source technologies.

PDF
Portable Document Format, a document format standard created by Adobe Systems, Inc. PDF has become a de facto standard for distributing documents in electronic format while preserving visual presentations usually reserved for printed content.

Photoshop
A robust image manipulation program produced by Adobe Systems, Inc.

QA
Quality assurance. The process of methodically testing and examining a product to determine if it meets predefined standards of quality and performance. Also called *quality control*. In the software industry, QA is a department or professional specialty.

RoboHelp
A help authoring tool produced by Adobe Systems, Inc. RoboHelp's most popular competitor is Madcap Software's Flare.

Screen capture

An electronic "picture" of part (or all) of what the user sees displayed on the monitor. Typically used to illustrate or supplement software or operating instructions.

Scrum

A variant of the Agile project management methodology.

SDK

Software development kit. A collection of software and tools designed to help programmers design and produce their own software. SDKs are often provided to help one program connect to another program.

Single-source publishing

The process of writing content once, then using software tools to publish it for multiple viewing methods (print, web, a help system, etc.)

Subject matter expert (SME)

A person with expert knowledge about a particular subject. Technical writers often rely on SMEs to help explain the technical subject they're writing about, and to help validate the information and assumptions contained in what they've written.

Society for Technical Communication (STC)

The most popular professional organization for technical writers, illustrators, and related professions.

Task analysis
The process of measuring and analyzing what tasks users do, how they do them, and related factors. Task analysis is typically used by technical writers to determine how best to write and present instructions.

Usability
A general term describing the "ease of use" of an object (like software); that is, how easy it is for a human to learn, use, and interact with an object.

User interface (or UI)
The part of a system that a human uses to interact with it. In software, the UI commonly refers to the visual aspect of a system (what is seen on a screen), but also can refer to the physical aspects of a system like the mouse and keyboard.

User-centered design
A general term for a philosophy that focuses the design process on the wants and needs of a system's user.

Version control
The management of changes to a document, program, or other object, usually with the aid of a software tool.

Web-based training (WBT)
Any learning system or learning content that I delivered via a web browser. uPerform and Captivate are two popular tools for delivering WBT.

White paper
A researched, authoritative document that describes how a product or process solves a specific problem. Typically used for marketing and decision-making purposes.